Marketing Untangled Series

Coming up in the series:

- make sure you don't miss them by signing up at thoranna.is/marketinguntangledseries

Target Groups Untangled:
The Small Business & Entrepreneur's Guide to Finding and Knowing Your Ideal Target Groups

Competition Untangled:
The Small Business & Entrepreneur's Guide to Knowing Your Competition

Branding Untangled:
The Small Business & Entrepreneur's Guide to Branding Your Business

Marketing Communications Untangled:
The Small Business & Entrepreneur's Guide to Choosing the Right Marketing Communications Tools

Marketing Systems Untangled:
The Small Business & Entrepreneur's Guide to Setting Up an Effective Marketing System

Marketing Untangled:
The Small Business & Entrepreneur's Map
Through the Marketing Jungle

by Thoranna Jonsdottir

DEDICATION

For Kalli, Ísold Saga and Ísak Máni,

who support me whatever I do.

CONTENTS

ACKNOWLEDGEMENTS

There are a few people who I would like to thank. First and foremost I would like to thank my husband and children, my parents and my little brother who always support me whatever I do. That's not a given, with all the stuff I get up to! Without them I don't know where I'd be.

To my fabulous clients throughout the years for appreciating this little marketing nerd. It is seeing your "aha" moments that makes me realize I can actually do this and seeing your success gives me the drive to keep doing this. Look forward to seeing you continue to kick ass!

Thanks to my dear friend Runa Magnus who has been my cheerleader all the way and a valued mentor and friend. Rúna—we did it, girl!

To Mummi whose designs always make me look like hot stuff—because you are a genius! Oh well, it runs in the family. ;)

Finally to my editor Rebekah, who helps me get the message out there in the most effective way possible. What a find you are. ;)

INTRODUCTION

Having worked with hundreds of entrepreneurs, startups and small business owners through my consulting business, lecturing, speaking, mentoring and online training program, I have found there is a clear path through the marketing jungle. This path consists of five elements. When worked in the right order and with a bit of effort, they will enable anyone to build a solid marketing program for their business, bringing good, loyal customers and the desired income.

This is neither astrophysics nor the reinvention of the wheel. Pick up any academic book on the subject, and you will find five key elements as the underlying theme:

- Knowing your target groups
- Analysing and monitoring the competition
- Building a strong brand
- Choosing the correct marketing communications
- Building a marketing system

However, they will take an awful long time to get to the point and kill you with academic jargon. ;)

Today's world is filled with shiny new things, gizmos and gadgets for marketing. The internet and social media has increased the size of our menu of ways to reach the target customer dramatically. There are also plenty of people out there telling you their versions of the secret to life, the universe and everything when it comes to marketing (of course as Douglas Adams taught us in *The Hitchhiker's Guide to the Galaxy*, the answer is 42). ;) I can tell you honestly, *there are no quick fixes.* There is no "just do this and you'll be rich" solution and anyone who tells you there is, is full of BS. You need to *do the work*—otherwise we'd *all* be rich, wouldn't we?

Do Facebook ads work? *Yes, if you know how to use them.* Does Twitter work? *Yes, if you know how to use it and put in the time.* Does SEO work? *Yes, if you do the groundwork.* All of these modern marketing tools and more are great—*if you know how to use them.* And knowing how to use them means having laid the groundwork through a solid marketing strategy. The fact is that it will always come down to the basics: the fundamental building blocks of an effective marketing program and the effort it takes to put it to work. *And they do work!* The basics that I want to outline in this book will untangle your marketing, and pave the way to a better business.

This book is the first in a series on untangling marketing for small businesses, and will give you a thorough overview of the process. The following books will delve deeper into each of the five basic elements.

To make sure you are notified when they become available, go to thoranna.is/marketinguntangledseries, leave me your name and email and I will be sure to let you know.

Can you relate to this?

I know you can. Most of us can. It's a crazy old world out there, a mess full of options and jargon. A complete jungle!

My aim is to get you from that to this:

In this book, I am giving you the map through the marketing jungle. So let's get started!

PLEASE NOTE: You can download a pdf of all images in this book larger and clearer for better viewing at thoranna.is/marketinguntangledbook

KNOW YOUR PEEPS

I know, everybody says it. *Know your customer.* Well, that's because it's true. We can't sell to everybody. We must find and focus on our target groups and once we have them covered, we may be able to expand them.

However, very few seem able to tell you how to find the ideal target group or groups for *you;* what exactly it is you need to know about your customers and how to find out. So I want to shed some light on that. Here are the main points to consider when it comes to knowing your target market:

The Helicopter View

It is important to get a good overview of your products, services, and the corresponding target groups. In many ways, improving your marketing efforts is more about getting organised than anything else. I find that housekeeping tasks are often the first things I need to go through with my clients.

I suggest mapping up products, services and target groups, looking at your products and services and the corresponding target groups on one hand, and on the other focusing on each target group and the products and services you can offer them. Knowing which target groups to target for each product or service will allow for more effective promotion of that product or service, and knowing which products or services are suitable for each target group will allow you to spot upselling and cross-selling opportunities.

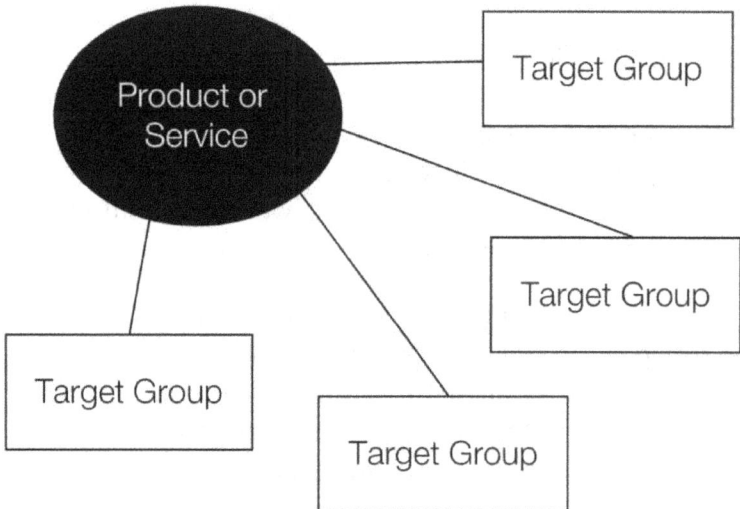

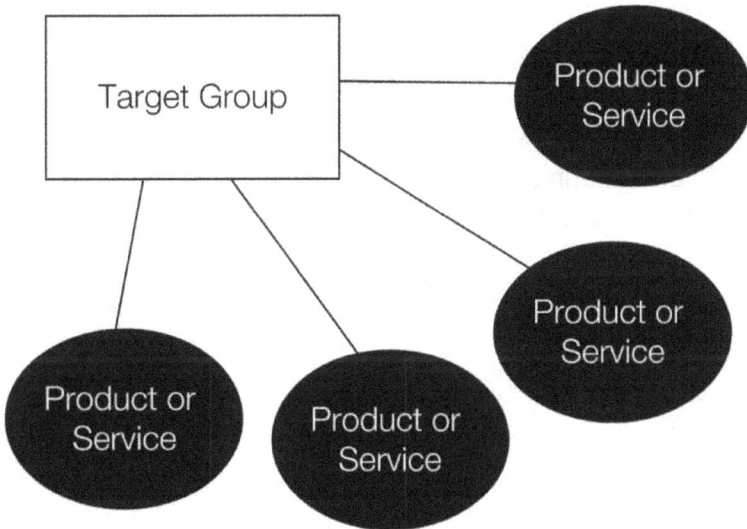

EXAMPLE: A client of mine runs a restaurant in the country, where she offers a range of services such as an *a la carte* menu, lunch buffet, meals for large and small groups, catering and annual events such as Thorrablot, an Icelandic midwinter feast.

Her target groups vary greatly, from local individuals or groups of friends and coworkers to Icelandic tourists. These target groups also include foreign tourists, either in tour groups or solo travellers.

Her *a la carte* menu aims to attract the following target groups:

- Locals
- Icelandic tourists travelling solo
- Foreign tourists travelling solo (may be further divided by nationality)
- Foreign tourists travelling within organized groups

The following services are offered to her local target group:

- *A la carte* menu
- Lunch buffet
- Group meals (e.g. for friends or coworkers)
- Event catering
- The restaurant's own events

Foreign tourists travelling in groups are offered:

- Lunch buffet
- Group meals
- Specially organised events for those particular groups

Find The Dream

People ask me all the time how to find their target market. If you are already in business, the best way to do this is by examining your existing clients to see which of them are your best customers. In a dream world, which ones do you wish all your customers were like? What do they have in common? Find the things which identify them, and then go out and find more people like that!

One of the biggest mistakes business owners make is trying to pander to the wrong customers. There *is* such a thing as bad customers. We all have them. The customer *isn't* always right! These are the ones who haggle on price, never pay on time and make unreasonable demands. Some of them are just plain rude and *all* of them are a general pain in the behind. I'm sure you know who I'm talking about. ;)

This makes everyone miserable. They're unhappy—not because of you, because they are probably just generally hapless—and there's nothing you can do about it. However, *they* don't see that, so they will blame you for their unhappiness (because it's easier than realising their happiness is up to them). And they *will* talk about it, believe me! They will discuss it with their friends, family, co-workers, or generally anyone who will listen (and probably also those that don't want to). So not only are they a pain in the ass, and not only will they *not* be creating more business by recommending you, but they are set on sabotaging your business by badmouthing you to the world—through no fault of your own.

These customers are poison. Not merely by slagging you off to the world, but also because they are bound to affect *you,* no matter how hard you try not to let them. They will zap your energy and you will be stressed because of them and the constant hassle they bring. You would have to be a saint for this *not* to affect you in other things you do. This means when you are dealing with the good customers, who you love to do business with, you are tired, cranky and generally not in good form; so you risk those relationships as well! Not to mention the time and energy you waste on the difficult customers, which would be much better spent on the good ones. Not only is this good for business, but it will also make you more content.

It is hard enough to run a business, but if you must also deal with difficult customers, it can really wear you down. It's quite alright to just say: "Thank you very much for considering us. I think actually you might find that this other company would be a much better fit for you than we are." But be *polite* about it. Nobody needs to get hurt; just find a civilized way of moving them along. Fire your bad customers and make sure the signals you put out repel rather than attract them. Identify the good ones, their preferences, find more like them out there and put out the right signals to draw them in.

Who Is In Charge

Make sure you identify each and every one who influences the purchase decision so that you can evaluate whether you need to address that group directly. At the very least you need to be aware of them. Think about whose idea it is in the first place to buy something which solves the customer's problem or fulfills their needs. Then consider who influences the decision by providing their opinion and advice. Who actually *makes* the decision and then who takes out the wallet and pays. Finally, who uses the product or service. In some cases, it may not be the same party doing any of those things.

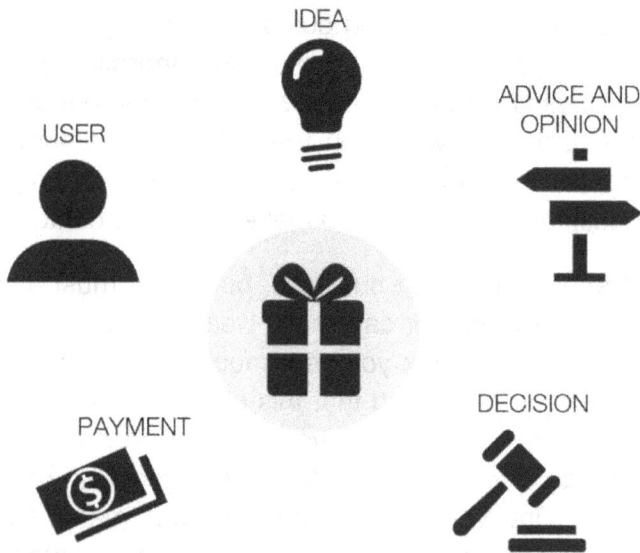

IDEA

ADVICE AND OPINION

USER

DECISION

PAYMENT

EXAMPLE: Buying breakfast cereal for the kids. They let daddy know he needs to pick up cereal. The parents try to follow advice from health gurus and child specialists to get something healthy—preferably oatmeal—while the children want that chocolate superhero cereal their friends have. Standing in the aisle, dad ultimately makes the decision to buy but at the counter mum pays for it. Once home, yes, the kids eat it—but dad loves to nibble on those chocolatey superheroes as well. ;) You must be aware of all these influences and of any spillover from the message going from one of those target groups to the others. If the children hear you talk too much about how healthy the oatmeal is, chances are they will instantly be against it. If the parents hear you talk too much about how sweet and chocolatey (and hence, bad for you) the cereal is, you will have them set against *it.* Tricky, isn't it?

You may find that you don't need to directly address each and every one of the target groups which affect the purchase decision, but you *do* need to be aware of them.

Don't Try To Conquer The World All At Once

You may find you have *loads* of possibilities when it comes to target groups. Don't be tempted to go for them all. Evaluate the most promising and focus on them *first.* We are all exposed to thousands of marketing messages each day, in addition to everything else in life. As a coping mechanism we continually sift through and choose what to pay attention to and what to shut out. Someone who isn't talking directly to *us*—and preferably *only* us—is *not* going to make the cut. You need to tailor the message and its communication to the people you want to reach as closely as possible, in order to have the best chance to cut through the noise and reach them. That's never going to happen if you try to talk to everyone. You don't have endless time and resources so make sure they're not wasted by spreading yourself too thin.

Start with one or only a few very promising target groups and focus on knowing exactly what they want and how best to reach them, and then go for it. Be patient; gradually your market will grow and you will gain the resources to service more of those target groups.

Define But Don't Box

You need to be able to define the target group or groups to focus on, but don't get hung up in old-fashioned boxes. Sure, some products and services are gender and age specific, but many are not. So rather than talking about men between the ages of 25-45 living in Liverpool with an undergraduate education and above average income, try to think in terms of lifestyle and values. *What matters to them? What do they love?*

EXAMPLE: Are they formal, suited and booted, classical music-loving guys, or are they jean-wearing, tattoo-sporting rockers?

Look at the women in the pictures. All these ladies could fit the same basic demographic and geographic definition. They might be the same age, married with two children, one at school and the other in kindergarten. They may all have a degree, earn a similar salary and live in the same neighbourhood. But do you think they all enjoy the *same things*? Or respond to the same type of messaging? Depending on what you are marketing, it is highly unlikely you can appeal or talk to all of them in the same way or in the same places and still get results.

Research has shown that grouping people by lifestyle and values is much more effective in reaching them and creating stronger customer relationships than the old boxes of age, gender, income brackets etc.

This Applies To Businesses As Well

Remember, even though you may be selling to other businesses (business-to-business or B2B market), at the end of the day you are still selling to *people.* So what kind of people are they? Your typical IT person is generally not like the general marketing person, are they? The more you can understand the individuals you are marketing to within the businesses and their needs, the better equipped you are to find the message that resonates with them the most.

Also, the businesses you serve may generally be a certain size, in specific industries etc., but this is not always the case. Consider their culture and character, their business values. Would you market to a groovy advertising agency in the same way as a formal government organisation? Probably (hopefully!) not. The company culture greatly affects what the most effective message and overall approach to that company is.

They Don't Give A S**t About You

Marketing is all about creating relationships that make people want to do business with you. Hmmm...so how can I talk about creating relationships and then say that people don't care about you? Well, because they *don't.* They don't care that your stuff has glitter and dancing monkeys. The only thing which matters is what it does for *them.*

What is in it for them?

You need to find out what their needs and problems are, then tell them how your product or service can fulfil those needs or fix those problems in a way that proffers the best fit for them. Now chances are others may be able to fulfil those needs or fix those problems as well, but you must convince them that *you* are the best option for them and the fact is, claiming to be the best overall, is *not* a viable strategy. Claiming to be the best for *them* or their particular situation may work however. Only if they think you are exactly the right business to help them will they start giving a s**t. And if you can fill that need or fix the problem to their satisfaction, they won't just give a s**t, they may just fall in love with you. ;)

Your Kind Of People

We all know there are *our* kind of people and then there are *other* kinds of people. That's just *life.* Find out who your kind of people are and make sure you are *their* kind in turn. What matters to them? What do they value? Is it money? Family? The environment? What are they passionate about? If you can find something in common, you are really on to something.

The strongest relationships are built on having the same outlook on life. Just think about the people in your circle and how you probably share values with the ones closest to you— your partner, your friends, your family—and find a way to create the alignment with your target market in that respect to form a stronger bond.

Where The Heck Are They?

All this stuff has been about identifying the best fit for you and getting to know them. But it doesn't do much good if you don't know where to find them. *So find out.* Where do they hang out? What do they read? Where are they online? What social media and websites do they use, etc. This is just nitty gritty research. And always remember, if you assume you know things, you are only making an ASS-of-U-and-ME. ;)

Market research does not need to be a major project or even mega expensive. Talk to people, observe them, do online surveys—there are many simple, affordable ways to gather the information you need.

Then go join them where they are—and where they don't mind having you around.

But remember, sometimes your product, service or message just doesn't fit the environment. So either don't be there, or adapt to make sure you *do* fit the environment. Facebook is a classic example. We use Facebook to socialise, so any marketing done on there needs to bear that in mind. Going on with a hard sell about something boring like say, plumbing, is probably not going to be very popular. I am not saying you can't use Facebook to market plumbing, but that you need to adapt to the environment. If you go for it, be prepared to shake it up a bit and make things fun in order to fit in. If you can't or won't, *don't go there.*

Make It Clear

Finally, you need to take all this information and communicate it clearly to the world. There are people who need to be able to understand exactly who your target groups are: your staff, customers, those you work with in marketing such as photographers, graphic designers, web designers, etc. If you can't boil all this down so they understand who they need to appeal to, they won't be able to help you reach them.

Create a clear stereotype for each target group. This makes things so much easier to communicate. This concept is sometimes called a "buyer persona" or "customer avatar". But whatever you call it, having it will make your life easier by allowing you to keep that stereotype in mind while writing a blog post, showing it to the graphic designer so they understand exactly who the designs must appeal to, or your advertising agency so they know exactly who the ads need to reach.

Want to delve deeper into determining and analysing your target groups?

Go to thoranna.is/marketinguntangledseries to be notified of my upcoming book on exactly that!

KNOW THY ENEMY

"So it is said that if you know your enemies and know yourself, you can win a hundred battles without a single loss."

—The Art of War by Sun Tzu

Okay, I am not saying the competition is necessarily your actual *enemy*. The quote from Sun Tzu just sounds really cool—and is spot on with the knowledge thing. You do need to know your competition. Why? There are a lot of reasons, but really only one merits mention: *When people ask why they should do business with you rather than the competition, how will you answer?*

If you don't know your competition you can't answer that question. And if you can't answer, then why on earth should they do business with you? You need to know and understand your customers' options so that you can guide them to the realisation that *you* are the best option for them.

Almost without exception, I meet resistance from my clients when it comes to analysing the competition. "I know these guys. I don't need to study them especially." Yet once they have done so, they come to me all revved up and raring to go because they have learned so much and uncovered so many opportunities.

Go out there and find out all you possibly can about the competition. Check out their website. Google them. Follow them on social media, sign up for their mailing list and set up a Google Alert for them. Look at what they have to offer and how they market their products and services. What is their flagship product or service? How do they differentiate themselves in the market? Are they going for price leadership or quality leadership? What is their pricing structure like? etc. etc. etc.

What can you learn from them, both good and bad? Can you borrow from their positive ideas? Are they making mistakes you should avoid, errors which may even create an opportunity for you?

In this age of endless information, you simply cannot say you're unable to learn about the competition, so go and find out, and then keep monitoring them regularly!

Want to delve deeper into competitor analysis?

Go to thoranna.is/marketinguntangledseries to be notified of my upcoming book on exactly that!

BE SOMEBODY

Seth Godin is quoted in a 2007 issue of *Forbes* as saying:

"Often a small business will run into problems, when the owners don't take that time early on to understand and build their individualized brand ... Small businesses become bigger when their marketing strikes a chord. They fail when they struggle to stay average ... if you build your brand right, you won't need to allocate more funds for marketing."

I could not agree more. A strong brand is your most effective marketing tool; it will amplify the effect of everything else in your marketing.

A brand is basically everything that people associate with you in their minds and hearts. When they hear the name of your brand, something specific comes to mind, even if they have never heard it before. Think about it; think of any word or name. Something will always come to your mind. There will always be an emotion attached to it. It may be weak, but it will be there.

EXAMPLE: Santa

We all know Santa, whatever our religious and cultural background. Santa is a good example of a very strong brand. We all have the same mental associations, largely built by Coca-Cola since the 1930's, and most of us have positive emotions towards him. In the image you can see some of those universal mental and emotional associations.

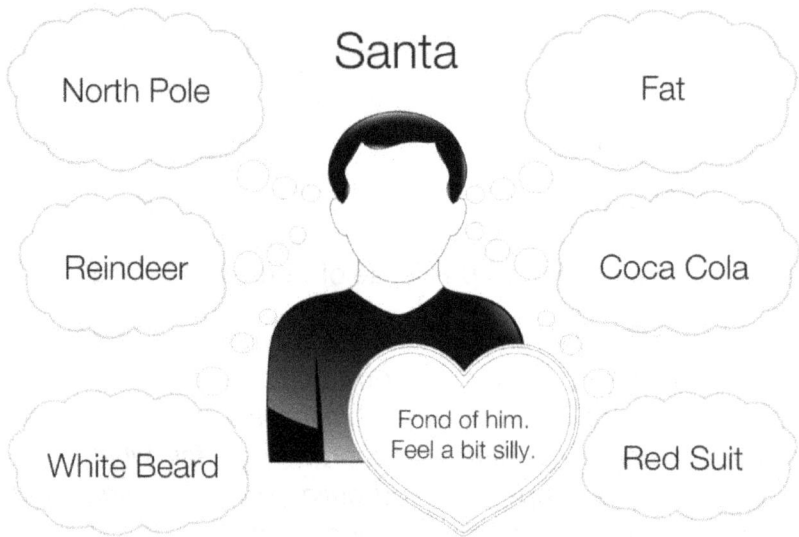

Then think about this: We buy based on *feelings.* Research has shown this again and again. We are not *rational* beings; our feelings guide us. At some point, our brains take over and we usually rationalize our purchase; sometimes before and sometimes after.

Your brand evokes thoughts and feelings, and those thoughts and feelings dictate whether we buy. Hence—your brand is the *single most important determinant* of whether people buy from you or not!

Upon hearing the word "brand" many people immediately think of logos and design, which is definitely part of a brand, just as the clothes people wear represent who they are as individuals. However, to say that a brand is *just* the logo and design is like saying a person is composed solely of her clothes, with nothing inside. A brand is the whole, the total being of your business, product, service, or you yourself as a small business owner or entrepreneur. It is the people's *experience* of *you.*

We all have a *brand,* whether we realize it or not. The mere mention of your business, product or service will conjure up some mental and emotional associations. It is crucial we don't leave it up to luck to determine what those associations are. We must take an active role in creating our brand in the minds of consumers to ensure that it will attract them to us and get them to buy.

Which leads me to another point: a brand is not what *you* say you are—it is what *they* say you are. Or as Jeff Bezos of Amazon fame so aptly put it: *"Your brand is what people say about you when you are not in the room."*

What do you want people to say about *your* business, product or service when you are not present?

How Do You Become Somebody?

Branding has long been considered the playing field of the big boys: the Coca-Colas, Nikes and Apples of the world. This is a huge misunderstanding; it does not take a lot of money or rare genius to build a brand. It does take a certain methodology, some patience and a good dash of courage. *The courage to be different and stand out!*

As we talked about in the beginning of this book, trying to be everything to everyone is not a proper business strategy, nor is it a good branding strategy. Standing out and daring to be different in a way that appeals to your target groups is an excellent strategy which will get you very, very far. Why do you think Lady Gaga, Madonna and Katy Perry are so famous? Their musical talent is no greater than many other artists. But their character and flamboyance—their *brand*—is, and that cuts through, creating division. Division between those that can't stand them, (which is fine, since they were probably never going to be won over anyway), and those that love them. And I mean *LOVE* them, hanging on their every word, buying absolutely every song and going to every concert they possibly can. The same laws apply to any other brand as they do those pop stars, because that is what makes big pop stars so successful: their incredibly big, brave and strong brands.

Want to explore some more brave brands, this time in business?

Check out my little ebook called "Stand Out By Being Brave" at thoranna.is/stand-out-be-brave

Building a brand involves several steps:

- If you are already in business, determine what your brand is today (what are they saying about you when you are not in the room? ;)
- Determine what you want your brand to be, taking into account
  - your target market and what will appeal to them
  - your competitors and how you plan to differentiate yourself from them
  - your *own* personality and company culture— *don't try to be something you are not*
- Examine the gap between the brand today and the brand you want to build and come up with a course of action to close that gap

- Determine every possible touchpoint with your brand
- Finally, build your desired brand consciously through each and every touchpoint

Once you have determined the brand you want to build, *be* that brand absolutely everywhere—through every possible touchpoint with the world no matter how big or small. Whether it be your retail space, offices, business cards, packaging, website, social media profiles or the way you conduct yourself, make sure each and every one of those points is building your brand. Only with a clear focus, consistency, and by constantly hammering in the same mental and emotional associations, can you build that brand in people's hearts and minds. That is what you must do to cut through the clutter and have a strong impact in the market.

Want to delve deeper into branding your business?

Go to thoranna.is/marketinguntangledseries to be notified of my upcoming book on exactly that!

CHOOSE THE RIGHT WAYS TO COMMUNICATE

Only when you are clear on your target market and the brand you want to build, can you begin choosing the marketing activities to construct that brand, and communicate with your audience. Should you be on Twitter, advertise in this magazine or that newspaper, or send out flyers? Whatever you do must be determined by four things:

- Target market
- Brand
- Yourself
- And creating a system which leads to the sale and beyond

Be Where Your Peeps Are

It seems straightforward enough, doesn't it? As we talked about before, be where you can reach your target market.

We talked about Facebook before and the need to fit into the social nature of the medium. Being on Facebook is a bit like being at a party and you need to fit in there. Another example could be LinkedIn, which is not a place to party. Don't get me wrong, there's no need to be boring, but you do need to be more professional and it's probably not the right place to be marketing your condoms or cupcakes with cat memes or crazy viral stunts. ;)

Be Aware Of Your Surroundings

The environment in which you reach your target groups will affect your brand. Make sure the mental and emotional connections they bring are positive. You may find media or places where you know your target market hangs out, but do they fit *your* brand? Tabloids are a good example. They may have a lot of readership, but if you want your brand to be classy and sophisticated, you don't want the brand association that a tabloid ad may bring.

Also, present yourself in the appropriate way for where you are. As with the examples above, if you are on Facebook, be fun, interesting and sociable. On LinkedIn, you can be a bit more serious and professional. But I must confess I hate when people think being likeable and fun means one is less professional or trustworthy. This is *not* the case; all it means is we get a lot of boring, faceless and heartless businesses. Similarly, do not place the same ad in a tabloid as the one you put in the *New York Times* or *The Guardian.*

You Matter

When you are Coca-Cola or Unilever, you can afford to just go for the marketing activities you want. If they don't have the knowledge and resources inhouse, they either hire in and buy stuff, or outsource. But when you are an entrepreneur, startup or small business you usually don't have that luxury.

When choosing your marketing approach, think on whether you have the knowledge and skills *within* the company; if you do, *use them*. Is there a good writer for that blog? Or someone photogenic and a good speaker to do that video? Or another employee who knows how to edit them? Do you have the money to pay for help from the outside to teach you or your staff their methods, or even do things for you? And if you *can* find someone to teach you or your staff, are any of you actually *interested* in learning?

It may be that a certain activity is perfect for your market and your product/service, but if you don't have the knowledge, skills and resources for it, go to the next best thing on the list. Further, do you—or the individual within your business who will be performing the task—actually *enjoy* it? Because if you're not keen on writing a blog, you won't do a good job. If you hate being on Twitter, you are not going to get positive results, etc. *If it doesn't float your boat, don't do it!*

Lead Them To Water And Make Them Drink

The fourth thing you need to determine which marketing activities you should use, is effectively building a system that leads people towards buying from you and beyond. Folks need to go through a mental process before they are even willing to buy from you; I simply call it "The Marketing Process." We then need to ensure we have the tools to move them through this process to get the sale, a process generally referred to as "lead management."

Have a look at the illustration:

Now let's look at each of those in turn:

Awareness

Well, this seems obvious, right? If no one knows you exist, they're not going to buy from you, are they?

Have you ever bought one ad in a paper or on the radio—and nothing came of it? Most of us have. Here's the thing: There are a gazillion things out there every day fighting for our attention. One little ad in the paper just isn't going to cut it. Depending on which source you cite, people need to see you at least 5-16 times before they even *notice* you! And some things we just never notice at all.

A strong brand will help cut through the clutter and get you that awareness by standing out and being interesting. This is also something a good ad, in the right place, repeated often enough, might help you achieve. Personally, I'm a big fan of

Facebook ads because you can get fantastic results for very little money, but that only works if you really know your target groups. There are various ways to do it—social media, PR etc. Just make sure you have specific marketing activities to get attention, awareness and be remembered. And whatever you do, don't ever think that once is enough.

Interest

We see and notice things all the time. That doesn't mean it goes any further. If we are not interested, things just stop there. So we need to make sure we are catching our target group's interest. Who cares if the others aren't interested? That is fine, but our target market must be engaged in order to take it further.

If you don't know your audience well enough, there is no way you can know what will pique their curiosity and push them to actually give you the time of day. Your message will be ineffective and lame; this is yet another place where a strong brand is invaluable and, by definition, *interesting.* Boring brands are weak. With the multitude of products out there, it is easy to blend into the background so that even if they see you, it won't prompt them to take any sort of action towards learning more about you—let alone buying.

To continue with an earlier example, whatever you think of Lady Gaga, Madonna or Katy Perry, they can never be accused of being boring. Be brave, be bold, be different, and you are much likelier to gain the interest of your audience than by being beige. ;)

Incidentally, your website is useless until after this point. If they don't know you exist and don't care, they are not going to visit it.

Like

Now, I will never advocate for you to try getting *everyone* to like you, your business, product or service. That is simply *not* going to happen. However, you do have to ensure your ideal target groups like you; the simple fact is, *we don't buy from businesses we don't like.*

Have you ever been into a store, already decided on a purchase, then actually turned around without buying, only to go buy the same thing somewhere else? Simply because there was just something you didn't like about the store, the salesperson, the parking lot or whatever? Be honest; most of us have. Many of us have even taken the time, and petrol to drive across town for that same item, even paying a little bit more for it.

You need to get your people to *like* your business, product or service. It is the same as with personal relationships; it means giving them attention, caring what they think, listening, helping and doing things for them, giving them things of value.

Content marketing (see thoranna.is/contentmarketing for more on that) is brilliant for this (and for a lot of other aspects of the marketing process). By giving your peeps valuable and intriguing content, helping them and enlightening them, you not only get them to like you, but as a bonus, you also create better informed customers who are a joy to serve.

Trust

There can be no business without trust; there must always be some level of it. It may just be a packet of chewing gum which doesn't cost me very much, but I still must be able to trust it doesn't contain anything toxic, or that it won't end up making my mouth blue for the rest of my life. ;) Granted, in that case the risk is generally fairly small but as things become more expensive or require more commitment, the greater the trust we must have in products and services before we buy.

There are a number of ways to build trust. Yet again, the brand plays a large role and may provide strong signals to consumers that you are trustworthy. In this instance the brand identity (or "brand clothes" if you will) can make or break that trust factor. Useful, detailed information on your website or packaging, ensuring customer service staff have all the information required, a solid LinkedIn profile with proper information, endorsements and recommendations... the list goes on and on. Just make sure you think about this through every marketing activity, so you are not missing a chance to build the trust which is necessary for business.

Trial

Even though we may "pretty much" trust someone, we are always going to want to try things out if we possibly can. We want to make sure those products are right for *us*. We also constantly perceive some risk in purchasing, however small the purchase may be; it is just human nature.

If you are selling a tangible product, it's usually fairly easy to give customers the chance to try it out. People can come into a store, handle the product, test it, or they can even buy it and then return it if they are not happy. That car can be test driven, and that cheap packet of gum costs so little that customers may not mind splashing out on it once to try it (but will not be buying it again if it's horrible).

If you are selling a service, this is trickier. It's simply the nature of the beast. If I go for that haircut, it can't very well be undone, can it? Once I receive that consultation, you can't really erase the advice from my mind, can you?

So you need to be a bit more creative in giving people a taste of what you offer. Can you provide them with a trial period, or convey the experience through a video? Can you explain your process so they know what to expect? Oh, and those case studies and testimonials everyone is talking about—yes, this is exactly where they come in handy.

Sale

If you have ever seen anything I do, or even if you have just been reading this book so far, you will know I am all about marketing; I do not stand for sales techniques and trickery. If you have a product or service which fills a need or solves a problem, and follow the marketing steps outlined in this book, your customers *will* come to you.

Peter Drucker put it perfectly: *"...the aim of marketing is to make selling superfluous. The aim of marketing is to know and understand the customer so well that the product or service fits him and sells itself. Ideally, marketing should result in a customer who is ready to buy. All that should be needed then is to make the product or service available."*

That being said, man is a creature of procrastination. Inertia is ingrained in our DNA. I keep seeing more and more that it is not necessarily the most clever individuals who achieve success, but rather the ones who take action. And the fact is most people simply *don't* act, they simply *don't* do. (Much like some of us don't do anything about our marketing and just hope business comes flooding in by magic. ;) So even though consumers are aware of your product or service, interested in it, like it, trust it and have even tried and love it—they still might not buy. In which case they need a little nudge.

You must have something in place which gets them to make a decision to buy now rather than leave it for later (and then forget it). The best ways to do this vary widely based on your product or service, how and where it is sold and a multitude of other things, but here are a few ideas to get you started:

- Give them a special deal only valid for a certain amount of time. Tip: giving them something extra is usually better than offering them a discount. That way they don't see the number on the price ticket going up again after the offer is finished, which is just more satisfying psychologically.
- Make sure they know what you are offering is brand spanking new—the latest version! Sorry, but we human folks are just suckers for that. If you doubt me on this one, just think of the lines outside Apple stores all over the world just before the release of a new iPhone which is really only marginally better than the one before. ;)
- Let them know about all the others who have purchased the product or service and are ecstatically happy with what it has done for them. Show them that they could be that happy customer too!
- Reduce their perceived risk. You can do this through detailed information, warranties, guarantees, return policies and more.

Repeat Sale

Here's another cliché we have all heard. The number varies depending on the source you cite, but basically it is about 10-16 times more cost effective to get your *existing* customer to buy more from you than it is to attract a new customer. And hey, considering all the steps people must go through in the marketing process before we actually get to the *sale,* this makes perfect sense.

Most of us however just cross our fingers and hope our customers are happy enough to return, leaving it up to luck. Think about this: *What can you do to encourage your existing customers to buy more from you?* How are you keeping in touch with them, building the relationship and loyalty? And how are you giving them the nudge to make additional purchases? *Don't leave it up to chance;* systematically go for the repeat sale.

Referrals

The final piece of the marketing process is referrals. Call it what you want, word-of-mouth, word-of mouse; we are simply talking about your customers creating more business for you by recommending your products and services to others and referring business.

This is another one where we tend to rely on Lady Luck and hope a happy customer spreads the news. *Why?* Think how you could actually encourage your customers to recommend you. Make it easy for them; even to the point of writing the referral for them and just asking them to send it to the right people.

If you do not actively have activities and processes in place to encourage referrals, you are leaving money on the table. This is one of the very few marketing activities which can actually cover the *whole* marketing process. Remember those ads we talked about? They can only do one thing at a time—and often don't even succeed at that one thing. A referral will drive people through awareness, interest, like, trust and even trial in one fell swoop, so the only thing you need to do is finish up the sale (and you may not even need that nudge). How? Well, picture this:

My friend Jane tells me she wants to get a business coach, and asks that I recommend someone. I choose to recommend my friend Joe. Here's what happens:

- Jane asked me to recommend someone, so she is going to be listening when I do. Instant awareness through one point of contact.

- Jane would not ask me about a business coach unless she was interested in getting one, and she would not ask *me* unless she cared about *my* recommendation. *Et voilà,* she wants to find out more about Joe.

- Jane would hardly ask me to recommend someone if she didn't like me. Then when I recommend Joe, Jane thinks: "Well, if Thoranna likes Joe, then I'll probably like him too."

- The same with trust: Jane would not ask for my recommendation unless she *trusted* me, and in turn I would only recommend someone I trust, so Jane's trust in me also transfers to Joe.

- Now, a recommendation is not a trial in itself. However, Jane is very likely to think, "Thoranna knows him and trusts him, and has probably tried his services, otherwise she would not recommend him, so I might as well just go for it." This won't necessarily happen; Jane may still want a trial session, but she will be much more positive going into that trial because I referred Joe, than if she didn't know him from Adam.

- Further, the sale may take an additional small nudge or it may not, but it *will* definitely be a lot easier than if Jane had learned about Joe through other marketing channels.

Now, here's the rub. Many of us are uncomfortable asking for referrals; we feel as though we are begging. The fact is, however, that if you offer a good product or service that your customer is happy with, they are *more* than willing to tell the world about *you.* Many even feel good about being able to recommend things which could help others—it is like a gift they can give to their friends and family. In a business environment in particular, if you refer positive things to your network, people begin to consider you a "go-to person" who is always helping by pointing them towards useful things. Therefore, they will be more willing to refer business to you, creating a circular win-win situation for all.

Lead Management - Sorry For The Jargon ;)

The marketing process outlined above is built from the potential customer's point of view. They are the ones who need to be aware, interested, like, trust, try, buy, return for more purchases, and refer. We can also look at this from our side, based on the tools we require to move them through that process. In marketing jargon (which I hate!), this is referred to as "lead management." A lead is the person who comes into the marketing process; we want to manage that lead through the process. Just to offer a different perspective, I want to look at the process from the lead management side.

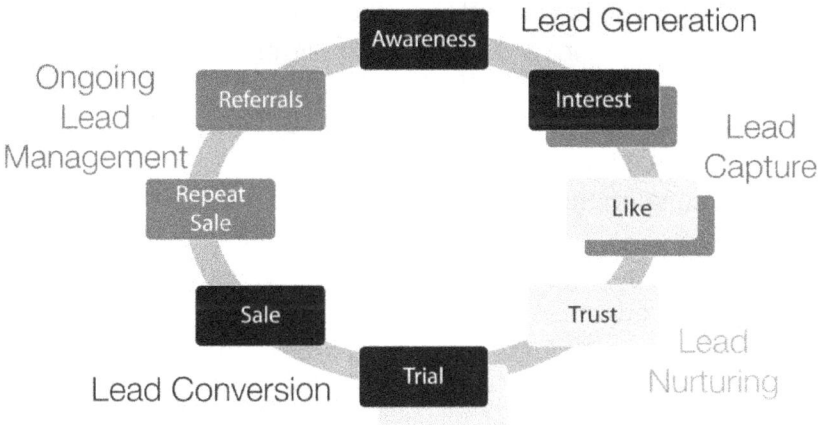

- **Lead generation** tools are the marketing activities responsible for creating awareness and interest. You can often use the same type of marketing activities for these purposes.

- **Lead capture** tools are the marketing activities that capture the person into the process. This is very difficult to do with traditional marketing methods, but much more efficient online where you would use specific capture pages and mailing list signups to "capture" the person into your marketing process.

- **Lead nurture** involves building your relationship with the potential customer. This is not "going for the sale" kind of stuff, but merely warming up for that. Here we encourage the "like" factor, build trust and get people to try out our products or services. Email marketing can be particularly strong in this area, as it is an affordable platform you can control. Advertising, social media and many other ways can be used, but are generally much more expensive and hit and miss with regards to reaching the individuals you are targeting.

- **Lead conversion** would be that nudge to get the sale. Often a trial is very closely connected to successfully persuading the person to buy.

- **Ongoing lead management** is snaring the desired repeat purchase and referrals. This may be done in various ways. Again, email marketing has proven to be very strong, but so are loyalty programs, referral programs and more.

Patience Is A Virtue

To sum it up, it takes a lot of work to get through the marketing process to the sale, and you must repeat the same message over and over and over again to ingrain it in consumers' minds. You also need to ensure one marketing activity leads to another. *EXAMPLE:* Say you have an initial ad on Facebook which takes people to your landing page, wherein they sign up for emails. You use these emails to build the relationship, get them to visit your webpage and sales page, where they finally buy—then keep in touch through email where you offer complimentary products/services. Then you ask them if there is anyone else that may like your product or service. Here is a referral.

There is a fantastic quote from Thomas Smith in 1885 on how often a man needs to see an ad before he buys:

1. *The first time a man looks at an advertisement, he does not see it.*

2. *The second time, he does not notice it.*

3. *The third time, he is conscious of its existence.*

4. *The fourth time, he faintly remembers having seen it before.*

5. *The fifth time, he reads it.*

6. *The sixth time, he turns up his nose at it.*

7. *The seventh time, he reads it through and says "Oh brother!"*

8. *The eight time, he says "Here's that confounded thing again!"*

9. *The ninth time, he wonders if it amounts to anything.*

10. *The tenth time, he asks his neighbour if he has tried it.*

11. *The eleventh time, he wonders how the advertiser makes it pay.*

12. *The twelfth time, he thinks it must be a good thing.*

13. *The thirteenth time, he thinks perhaps it might be worth something.*

14. *The fourteenth time, he remembers wanting such a thing a long time.*

15. *The fifteenth time, he is tantalized because he cannot afford to buy it.*

16. *The sixteenth time, he thinks he will buy it someday.*

17. *The seventeenth time, he makes a memorandum to buy it.*

18. *The eighteenth time, he swears at his poverty.*

19. *The nineteenth time, he counts his money carefully.*

20. *The twentieth time he sees the ad, he buys what it is offering.*

Now, if he figured this out in *1885,* why are many of us *still* making the mistake of thinking that occasional fireworks here and there will do the trick? You can clearly see now that it is not just a question of an ad here or a Facebook status there. You need to build a system of marketing activities that work *together,* much like you need to tune *together* the various instruments of a band to make music and then keep playing constantly!

Want to delve deeper into choosing the right communications tools for your business?

Go to thoranna.is/marketinguntangledseries to be notified of my upcoming book on exactly that!

OK, SO IT'S NOT SEXY

Here's the thing. I know that marketing has an image of creativity and wildness, particularly when looking to advertising agencies. It is, and it can be, and creativity is definitely likely to produce some great stuff. The fact of the matter is, however, that when you are a small business, something very creative and exciting may not be constantly sustainable. If we feel like everything we do in our marketing needs to be a huge firework display, it becomes too hard, discouraging us, so in the end we don't do anything at all.

Like so many others, I am a perfectionist. I say this not to blow my own trumpet; I don't even say it as a good thing. The problem with perfectionists is they don't get things *out there;* very often nothing really happens. This book, for example, has been way too long in the works, until I decided that this was *it,* I just had to *go* for it! There really is no such thing as perfect, and I'd rather get out there and do things than sit at my desk perfecting something that will never be perfect anyway. I want to help people improve their marketing, and this book is not really going to help anyone unless I get it out there, will it? ;)

When it comes to marketing, constantly working at it and getting things out there is *key* so we must not get hung up in perfectionism. *Things do not happen by themselves; we need to make them happen.*

Remember that marketing process. It takes an awful lot of contact with people to move them through that process, so an occasional firework display is just not going to cut it. Although brilliant things are great, it is much better to do average things consistently than just produce brilliant material once in a blue moon.

Martin Lindström likened staff brand training to spinning plates at the circus: once you think the plates are going to continue to spin and you stop checking on them, they will start to wobble and, if not tended to, will eventually begin to drop. Marketing to your potential customers is the same. You need to keep spinning those plates, checking on each of them regularly and giving them a nudge so they won't wobble and fall.

Now here's another problem. When you are running a small business, you are bound to wear *many* hats. There is customer service, the books, production, development, website updates, etc. The only way you are going to get it all done—*and* constantly keep your marketing going—is by getting organised and setting up a system.

In my training, I get all my clients to make a list of everything they need to do in their marketing, whether it is one-off projects like setting up a website, regular events such as trade shows or sales, or recurrent internal events like reviewing their target groups, competitor analysis, brand strategy or marketing program. They also document things such as weekly social media scheduling, goals for obtaining media coverage, etc. etc. Absolutely *anything* and *everything* they need to make sure gets done in their marketing. Then they get out their calendar, enter those pesky little things in there, *AND STICK TO IT!* *Don't let the urgent stuff get in the way of the important stuff!*

It is marketing that gets customers and customers who create revenue; without revenue, your business will die! *Now* do you think doing your marketing is worth it?

Put It In Writing!

Another thing to do is set up checklists and processes.

There are bound to be a number of things in your marketing which you do over and over again. There may be sales at regular times throughout the year, you may always attend an annual conference or have a booth at a specific trade show, or you may host the same event year after year. Do you still find yourself running around like a headless chicken just before the event starts or you open the doors to that sale, forgetting things and generally going crazy? *Why do we do this to ourselves?*

Write things down. Make checklists and keep them organised. When you need to begin preparations, make sure your calendar lets you know. Then simply refer to your list and get to work. The number for your graphic designer: in the list; the number of brochures printed for last year's conference: in the list, etc. Not only does it make things easier for you by ensuring you do things in a timely manner, have all the necessary information and don't forget details, there is another huge benefit to it:

Have you ever asked for someone's help with a project, and then once you start explaining to them what to do you simply gave up saying, "Oh, it'll be quicker if I just do it myself?" It takes time to explain things, giving people all the information they may need. But what if you could just hand them a piece of paper saying, "Could you please help me with this? All the information is here, give me a shout if you have any questions or need any help." *Wouldn't that make life just a little bit easier?*

How's It Going?

How's it going? Good? That's great! *How do you know?*

You must be clear on what you want your marketing activities to do and how you are going to know whether they are doing it or not. For my part, and for all of the small business owners and entrepreneurs I know, we don't have the time or resources to be doing things that don't work. I'm sure you don't either. The only way to make sure you are not wasting your efforts is to measure your results.

Go through each and every marketing activity you are using, and figure out what you want it to accomplish. Think about the marketing process and lead management. How can you measure whether it's working? If it isn't, what are you going to do about it? You either figure out a way to fix it, or you drop it. If it's working, great; *do more of it!* You work too hard on your business for your marketing not to work as hard—and preferably harder—than you.

Want to get your marketing organised and set up a system?

Go to thoranna.is/marketinguntangledseries to be notified of my upcoming book on exactly that!

CONCLUSION: GOOD BEGINNING MAKES A GOOD ENDING

A good beginning makes a good ending. Now this may not *always* be true, but it sure as heck increases the *likelihood* of a good ending. ;)

I know for a fact if you build a strong foundation for your marketing—with a clear view and understanding of the target market, detailed knowledge of your competitors, a strong brand, well-chosen marketing activities which support each other and move people through the marketing process, and take care of marketing your business in an organised and consistent fashion—this will all yield *great* results. Yes, those Facebook ads may be fantastic, and sure, that Canva tool is really cool, but if you don't have the basics in place, it's like expecting to win a race because you have a fancy car—even if you have never learned how to drive. Please don't. ;) Apart from probably killing yourself, you're never going to win. There are no quick fixes. There are no shiny fancy tools to do it for you. *You've simply got to pay your dues and do the work; and then you will reap what you sow.*

If you are interested in diving deeper into any of the aspects of the marketing map, make sure you follow me to learn when my in-depth books are out!

Currently in the works are five books, on each section of the map: your target groups, competition, branding, marketing communications and the marketing system.

Sign up and be the first to know when each of them is available—and as an early bird you may even be able to grab your copy for free! ;)

Go to: thoranna.is/marketinguntangledseries

In the meantime, have a look at your marketing activities. Implement the advice outlined in this book and please tell me what you think of all this.

My passion is to help entrepreneurs and small business owners build businesses that people love. Businesses that customers love and businesses that owners and entrepreneurs love running. I want to help you realise your dream. We go into business to fulfil some dream, whether it be independence, being liberated from the boss, helping people, changing the world or making your own money. Whatever motivates you to run your business, there is a dream in there somewhere. It breaks my heart that so many businesses never realise their vision, in large part because they fail at marketing. *Marketing is just that important; it* is more often than not what makes or breaks a business. That's why I want to help you master your marketing, so that *you* can fulfil *your* dream and build a business that people will love.

Finally - come and join me in the Marketing Untangled Series Facebook group (facebook.com/groups/MarketingUntangledSeries/) where we talk marketing and I pop in regularly to join the discussion and answer your questions.

Here's to your marketing success!

XO

Thoranna

P.S. This is *not* an academic book. It is designed to be accessible to non-marketing specialists and non-academics. Therefore I have neither filled it with references nor do I have a bibliography here at the end. It is however firmly based in academic research and practical knowledge. On thoranna.is/booksandresources you can find information about the books and resources which underpin my writing and all my work. The same page offers additional interesting resources as well; I encourage you to check them out to learn more and open up your marketing world. ;)

ABOUT THE AUTHOR

The Marketing Strategy Nerd from Iceland—helping build businesses people *love!*

Thoranna has worked in marketing since the beginning of the 21st century, with global advertising agencies Publicis and McCann Erickson, and within the finance and IT industries. Soon after the 2008 economic collapse she started her own marketing consultancy working with startups and small businesses. Her passion for helping entrepreneurs, extensive speaking experience and media appearances give her a unique perspective on providing jargon-free practical advice for non-marketing specialist clients. Thoranna holds an MBA with Distinction from the University of Westminster in London.

Thoranna lives in Iceland with her husband and two children. Before starting her career in marketing she trained for musical theatre, subsequently working as an actress and singer. Being too straight for the bohemian life (and today probably often too wild for the business world ;) she toured the United Kingdom with the *Rocky Horror Show,* even meeting the legendary Richard O'Brian, before doing a 180-degree turn into the business world and is constantly amazed at how much her former life helps her and her clients in business!

Find out more at thoranna.is and on social media:

Facebook.com/thoranna.is

Twitter.com/thoranna

LinkedIn.com/in/thorannakristin

Pinterest.com/thoranna

Plus.google.com/+ThorannaIsMarketing